Motorbikes

FOR SALE

WITHDRAWN FROM STOCK

Lisa Jane Gillespie

Designed by Anna Gould

Illustrated by Emmanuel Cerisier, John Fox, Adrian Dean and Adrian Roots

Edited by Alex Frith and Jane Chisholm

Motorb... ...: Museum
and Neil Syming... ...vel and Transport

Contents

Bikers kick up mud as they scramble around the first corner of the British Motocross Championships, 2009.

Which bike?

Motorbikes are fast, powerful and easy to manoeuvre. Some are built for speed; others for style – but they all have the same basic parts.

Mirror

Handlebar: for steering

Frame: the metal skeleton of the motorbike

Fork: connects the front wheel to the frame

Tyre: grips the road

Street bikes are mass-produced, affordable bikes suited to city travel.

Choppers are long bikes stripped of many panels and most decoration.

Engine: powers the motorbike

Saddle: where the biker sits

Exhaust: carries away waste gas

The fastest road motorbike in the world is called a Ducati Desmosedici RR. It can reach a top speed of 320km/h (200mph).

Cruisers are stylish street bikes that are often colourful and personalized, based on old, classic bike styles.

Sport bikes are built for speed. They're made of light materials and have powerful engines.

Touring bikes have strong engines and large fuel tanks for long distance rides.

Dirt bikes are used for racing on off-road tracks of grass, sand, ice and mud.

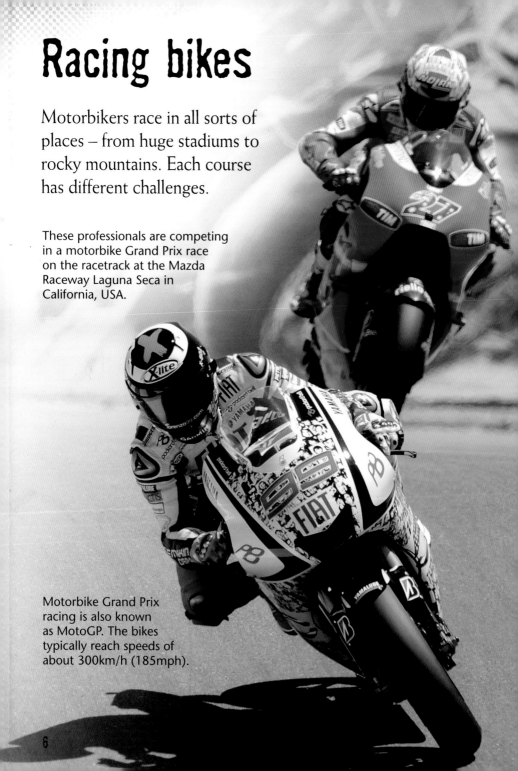

Racing bikes

Motorbikers race in all sorts of places – from huge stadiums to rocky mountains. Each course has different challenges.

These professionals are competing in a motorbike Grand Prix race on the racetrack at the Mazda Raceway Laguna Seca in California, USA.

Motorbike Grand Prix racing is also known as MotoGP. The bikes typically reach speeds of about 300km/h (185mph).

Tricky terrains

Unlike most cars, motorbikes are so powerful and easy to manoeuvre that they can travel over different types of surfaces, or terrains, from rocky hillsides to riverbanks.

The first motorbikes were nicknamed 'mechanical horses'.

Water
This biker is powering through a river. The engine is high up so the water doesn't get in and damage it.

Right handgrip: twisting this operates the throttle, moving fuel from the tank to the fuel injection system.

Headlamp

Fork: attaches the front wheel to the frame. The handlebars steer the fork which steers the wheel.

Front suspension unit, called a telescopic fork suspension

The wheels are attached to the frame through suspension units. These contain springs that absorb the impact from bumps in the road. Find out more on page 22.

Front brakes

The tyres are made of tough rubber, fille with air, and fitted t the rims of the wheels.

The spoked wheels are made of steel or aluminium, to be as light as possible.

Handlebars: steer the bike. Find out more on page 21.

Right lever: squeezing this operates the front brake.

Left lever: squeezing this operates the clutch. The clutch controls the connection between the gearbox and engine.

Right pedal: operates the rear brake.

Left pedal: changes gears.

These bikes are being assembled in the Harley-Davidson Vehicle Operations department in Pennsylvania, USA.

Ice
Special spiked tyres stop the bike from sliding and falling over on icy surfaces.

Mountains
Bikers can steer around rocks on mountain terrain, and the bike's tyres grip the stones.

Mud
A car might sink into mud, but a motorbike is light and fast enough to travel through it.

Sand
Bikers can use special 'paddle' tyres for riding on sand. They're knobbly and don't get clogged up easily.

Safety gear

Bikers wear tough clothing and strong safety gear to protect themselves from injury in falls and crashes.

Most **jackets** are made from Kevlar, a man-made material that won't scrape or tear if the rider falls onto a rough surface at speed.

Shoulder and **spine padding** minimize the risk of breaking bones or bruising muscles.

Tough **gloves** protect the rider's hands from injury and the weather, but don't interfere with operating the controls.

Trousers made from Kevlar protect the rider's legs.

Riders wear **layers** under their outer gear – thermals to keep warm in the cold, or light layers of breathable fabrics to keep cool in the heat.

Strong, heavy **boots** protect the rider's ankles and feet but allow firm contact with the pedals.

Helmets

A biker's helmet is made of light, strong fibreglass and carbon fibre.

The visor protects the rider's face from bugs, dust and stones.

A casing inside the helmet protects the rider's head from knocks and bumps, preventing brain damage in case of a fall.

Knee and **elbow braces** – moulded pieces of plastic that slot around the joint – reduce the risk of breaking bones in a fall.

The engine

Inside motorbike engines are cylinders containing fuel, which is used to drive pistons up and down. This piston motion is what powers the bike.

How the engine works

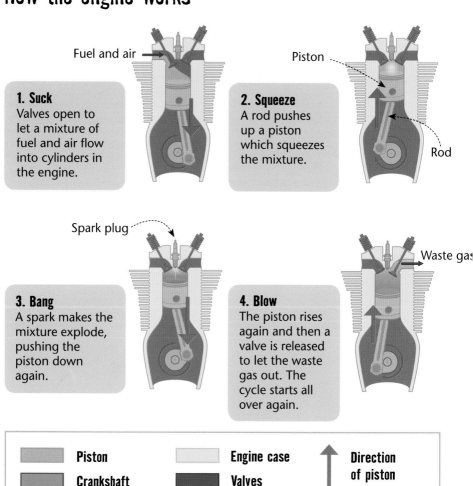

Fuel and air

1. Suck
Valves open to let a mixture of fuel and air flow into cylinders in the engine.

Piston

2. Squeeze
A rod pushes up a piston which squeezes the mixture.

Rod

Spark plug

3. Bang
A spark makes the mixture explode, pushing the piston down again.

Waste gas

4. Blow
The piston rises again and then a valve is released to let the waste gas out. The cycle starts all over again.

Piston	Engine case	Direction of piston
Crankshaft	Valves	

Turning the wheels

The movement of the pistons turns a piece of metal called the crankshaft. The crankshaft carries power to the gearbox, which turns the drive system. This powers the rear wheel.

	Engine case
	Cylinder
	Piston
	Crankshaft
	Gearbox
	Drive system

This engine is known as a V2 or a V twin, because it has two cylinders arranged in a V shape.

The front wheel spins freely, pushed forward by the engine driving the rear wheel.

As the pistons move up and down, they turn the crankshaft.

The gearbox controls the amount of power sent to the drive system.

This bike has a shaft drive system. This is a metal bar that pushes, pulls and turns to make the wheel go around.

Some motorbikes have chain drive systems which are similiar to chains on bicycles.

Engine layout

Engines can have anything from one to eight cylinders, arranged singly, in rows, or in V shapes. You can often tell how many cylinders an engine has because they're shiny and on show.

Here are four examples of the many possible engine arrangements:

Piston   **Crankshaft**

A **single cylinder** engine has only one cylinder and piston.

A **V2** engine has two cylinders at an angle to each other.

A **flat 4** engine has four cylinders in two rows that push in opposite directions.

An **inline 4** engine has four cylinders side-by-side in a single row.

Bike power

A bike's power is defined in *bhp* at *rpm*. *Bhp* stands for 'brake horsepower' and *rpm* for 'revolutions per minute' – the number of times a minute the crankshaft turns.

Brake horsepower compares the power of engines to the power of horses. It was invented when engines replaced horses for work and travel, so people could understand how powerful the engine was.

A dial on the bike's controls gives that moment's rpm reading. This dial shows 11,000rpm.

Comparing engines					
Motorbike	Weight	Cylinders	Capacity	Max. power	Top speed
Scooter	150kg (331lbs)	1	125cc	15bhp at 9,750rpm	100km/h (62mph)
Super bike	185kg (408lbs)	V2	1,150cc	150bhp at 10,000rpm	275km/h (171mph)
Cruiser	330kg (728lbs)	V2	1,720cc	74bhp at 4,500rpm	200km/h (124mph)
Sport bike	150kg (331lbs)	inline 4	790cc	200bhp at 23,000rpm	300km/h (186mph)
Touring bike	360kg (794lbs)	flat 6	1,850cc	120bhp at 5,500rpm	195km/h (121mph)
Dirt bike	96kg (212lbs)	1	250cc	40bhp at 13,500rpm	121km/h (75mph)

The number of cylinders and their arrangement differs from company to company.
For example, Harley-Davidson only uses V2 engines.

The total amount of fuel and air drawn into the cylinders during one engine cycle is known as the capacity. It's measured in cubic centimetres (cc).

In the saddle

Riding a motorbike takes concentration, care and co-ordination. A rider must balance, operate the controls and steer — all at the same time.

The rider of this powerful sport motorbike, a Suzuki GSX-R750, is leaning over to balance the bike, so it doesn't topple over as it turns the corner. He is leaning so far that his knee is almost touching the ground.

Motorbike controls

All bikes have the same controls, although they're not always in the same places. Here is a typical set of controls.

Tachometer: measures the rpm of the engine.

Speedometer: shows the speed of the bike.

Start button

Indicator button, to signal when turning

Kill switch: cuts the engine out in an emergency.

Clutch lever

Front brake lever

Horn

Gear pedal: to change gears, the biker moves the gear pedal up and down.

Ignition key

Twisting the **right hand grip** 'throttles' the engine, giving it more fuel so the bike goes faster.

Kickstand: to prop the bike up when parked.

Rear brake pedal

Foot pegs, to rest feet on during trip

Saddle

To slow down, the rider squeezes the front brake lever and presses the rear brake pedal at the same time.

Turning corners

Motorbikes need to be handled differently at different speeds. To turn a corner at low speeds, the rider turns the handlebars in the direction of the bend.

The biker leans over slightly with the bike to help balance it...

...and steers into the direction of the turn.

The rider turns the handlebars in the opposite direction to the bend...

...and leans strongly into the turn.

At high speeds, the rider turns the handlebars in the opposite direction to the bend. This is called counter steering. It's necessary because motorbike tyres spin very quickly and wobble a bit when the bike is moving fast.

Bumps and brakes

A motorbike relies on different systems working together to run smoothly. The two most important systems are the suspension and brakes.

Suspension　　　**Brakes**

How suspension works

Spring

Spring

Plunger

Swing arm

A swing arm is attached to the frame. A spring allows it to swing up and down gently to absorb shocks.

To absorb a shock, a plunger moves into a column of oil, then a spring returns it slowly to its original place.

How brakes work

Disc brakes

Drum brakes

Drum brakes expand and press against the rear wheel. This gently stops it turning.

Disc brakes pinch part of the front wheel. This quickly stops it turning.

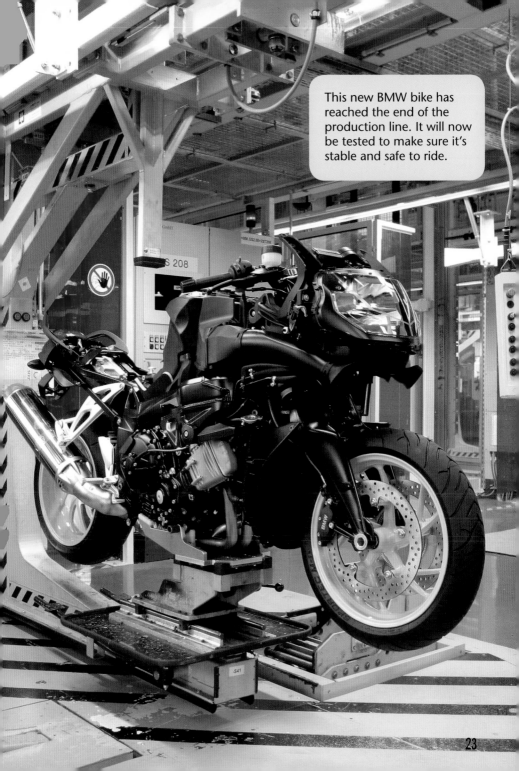

This new BMW bike has reached the end of the production line. It will now be tested to make sure it's stable and safe to ride.

Street bikes

Street bikes, sometimes called standard bikes, are the ones you'll see most often. With medium-sized engines, they're suited to city life and are often used as delivery bikes.

TDM900

(Yamaha Motor Company, Japan, 2010)

- **Engine:** 897cc, inline 2 cylinder
- **Weight**: 223kg (492lbs)
- **Power:** 86bhp at 7,500rpm

This is the usual riding position for a street biker.

Lights, mirror and a horn help the rider move through traffic.

A muffler fitted to the exhaust reduces its noise.

The tread patterns on the tyres allow them to grip dry and wet road surfaces well.

The frame is made from aluminium, which is strong and light.

F 800 R
(BMW Motorrad, Germany, 2011)

- **Engine:** 798cc, inline 2 cylinder
- **Weight:** 170kg (375lbs)
- **Power:** 86bhp at 8,000rpm

Splendor
(Hero Honda, India, since 1994)

- **Engine:** 97cc, single cylinder
- **Weight:** 109kg (240lbs)
- **Power:** 75bhp at 8,000rpm

Over 8 million Splendor bikes have been sold, making them the biggest-selling motorbikes ever.

Scooters have small engines. They're easier to learn to ride than bigger bikes.

Vespa GTS 125 Super
(Piaggio, Italy, 2009)

- **Engine:** 124cc, single cylinder
- **Weight:** 151kg (333lbs)
- **Power:** 15bhp at 9,750rpm

Touring bikes

Touring bikes were developed for long distance road trips across the USA. These heavy bikes have large fuel tanks, powerful engines, extra storage space and wide windshields.

VN1700 Voyager (Kawasaki, Japan, 2009)

- **Engine:** 1,700cc, V2
- **Weight:** 406kg (895lbs)
- **Power:** 74bhp at 5,000rpm

Touring bikes can easily carry passengers.

Aerial for radio

Room for two people to travel in comfort

Wide windshield

Huge headlights

Lots of space for luggage

GL1800 Goldwing
(Honda, Japan, 2001)

- **Engine:** 1,832cc, flat 6 cylinder
- **Weight:** 363kg (800lbs)
- **Power:** 117bhp at 5,500rpm

Honda Goldwings are often used as official vehicles for traffic police in the USA.

Sprint GT (Triumph, UK, 2011)

- **Engine:** 1,050cc, inline 3 cylinder
- **Weight:** 268kg (589lbs)
- **Power:** 128bhp at 9,200rpm

The GT in the Sprint's name stands for 'Grand Tourer'. These bikes can carry enough fuel for a 320km (200 mile) journey.

Electra Glide Ultra Limited
(Harley–Davidson, USA, 2011)

- **Engine:** 1,690cc, V twin
- **Weight:** 389kg (858lbs)
- **Power:** 78bhp at 3,500rpm

Emergency bikes

Some street and touring bikes have been adapted for use by police, paramedics and firefighters. They're fast and can dodge city traffic more easily than cars, ambulances and trucks.

This bike is used by the London Ambulance Service to rush to emergency situations.

Handlebars can be heated, so that paramedics have warm hands when they treat patients.

Rear emergency light

Blue, flashing emergency lights

Extra luggage boxes carry medical supplies.

A city-centre emergency

A fire breaks out in a narrow city-centre alley. Someone contacts the emergency services.

Rear emergency light

Hose reel

Water and foam canisters

The fire brigade decides to send a fire bike.

The firefighter speeds to the emergency.

The bike carries a long hose and canisters containing water and foam. First the firefighter sprays water, then switches to the foam to extinguish the flames fully.

Cruisers

Cruisers have the style and feel of old classic bikes (see pages 72-73), but with powerful, modern engines.

Blackline (Harley-Davidson, USA, 2011)

- **Engine:** 1,584cc, V twin
- **Weight:** 294kg (648lbs)
- **Power:** 75bhp at 3,250rpm

Cruiser riders sit upright with their arms up, and usually their feet in front of them.

Large headlight

Low saddle

Sleek-looking dual exhaust pipe

Footrest

Exposed engine

Commando 961SE (Norton, UK, 2010)

- **Engine:** 961cc, inline 2 cylinder
- **Weight:** 188kg (414lbs)
- **Power:** 80bhp at 6,500rpm

The Commando is sometimes described as a café racer. It's based on a style of 1960s racing bike.

Chief Classic (Indian, USA, 2010)

- **Engine:** 1,721cc, V2
- **Weight:** 330kg (728lbs)
- **Power:** 74bhp at 4,500rpm

Indian Motorcycles have been making Chiefs since 1920. They're among the best-loved American bikes.

VT750C Shadow (Honda, Japan, 2010)

- **Engine:** 745cc, V2
- **Weight:** 252kg (555lbs)
- **Power:** 45bhp at 5,500rpm

Choppers

Choppers are powerful, large, stretched-out bikes. They are sometimes called stripped-down, or naked, bikes because they often have no panelling, mirrors, windshields or mudguards.

Personalized mirrors

This chopper was specially designed and built for a customer.

Wide handlebars

Stylish flame red with decoration in places

Very low saddle

Extra wide rear wheel

Double exhaust

V2 engine, shiny and on show

Chopper riders lean back with their arms and legs stretched out.

The name 'chopper' was first used in the 1950s, when bikers used to chop off unwanted parts of their bikes to make them lighter and faster.

Old fashioned headlight

No mudguard

Large front wheel

Long fork

Panelling has been removed so the frame is visible.

Many chopper riders build their own customized motorbikes from scratch.

Personalized chrome spokes on front wheel

Sport bikes

Sport bikes are designed to be among the sleekest, fastest and most powerful vehicles on the road.

Huge fans create winds of up to 499km/h (310mph).

This sport bike is being tested in a wind tunnel. This simulates high-speed riding conditions to test how aerodynamic it is – how smoothly it moves through the air.

These orange leads are electrical sensors that help engineers examine how wind moves around the bike.

The tyres run on treadmills that keep the bike in position. Speed readings are sent to a computer for analysis.

Sport bike riders sit with their hands and head leaning forward and their legs tucked behind them.

Ninja ZX-RR (Kawasaki, Japan, 2009)

- **Engine:** 798cc, inline 4 cylinder
- **Weight:** 148kg (326lbs)
- **Power:** 200bhp at 22,916rpm

Daytona 675 (Triumph, UK, 2010)

- **Engine:** 675cc, inline 3 cylinder
- **Weight:** 185kg (408lbs)
- **Power:** 124bhp at 12,600rpm

Isle of Man TT

One of the biggest sport bike events is the Isle of Man Tourist Trophy (TT), which is held every year. It is a time trial race: the competitors ride in groups, each trying to complete the course in the fastest time.

The TT is a road race – public roads are closed to cars and pedestrians during the race.

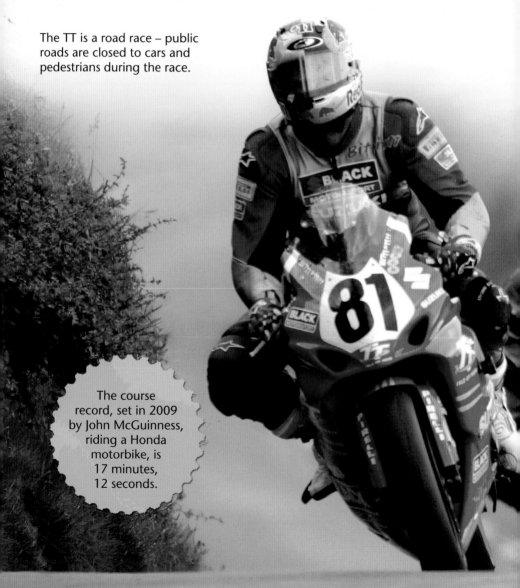

The course record, set in 2009 by John McGuinness, riding a Honda motorbike, is 17 minutes, 12 seconds.

The competition lasts about two weeks, with practice runs, heats and finals for each size of engine.

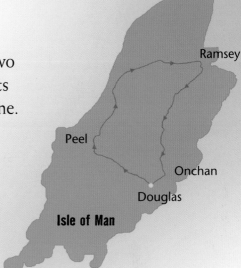

Ramsey

Peel

Onchan

Douglas

Isle of Man

Fans line much of the route to watch the racing. This can be dangerous if a rider crashes into the race barriers.

Each race starts and finishes in the town of Douglas. The course is 60km (38 miles) long and covers towns and countryside, mountain roads and many sharp bends.

Rider Joey Dunlop won the TT a record 26 times. He died during a race in Estonia in 2000.

Superbikes

The most powerful, high-tech bikes, with capacities of around 1,000cc or more, are known as superbikes. They are very expensive because engineers spend years designing them.

Superbike riders sit in the same position as sport bike riders.

This rider is racing during the 2008 Superbike Supersport World Championships in Doha, Qatar.

Some superbikes are built to ride on public roads; others are only raced in competitions. Only bikes designed for the track are raced in MotoGP events, while modified versions of road superbikes are raced in the Superbike World Championships.

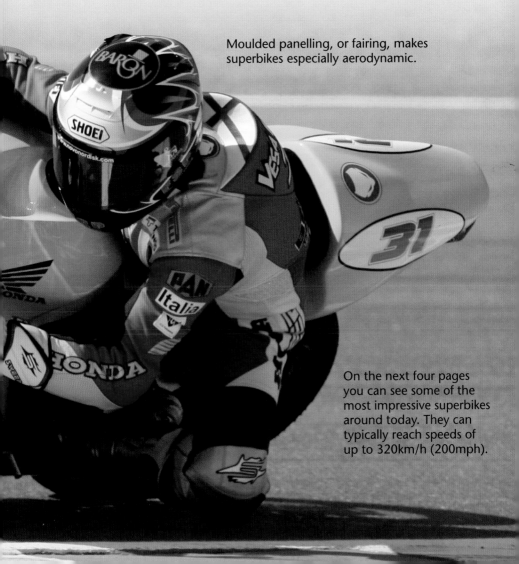

Moulded panelling, or fairing, makes superbikes especially aerodynamic.

On the next four pages you can see some of the most impressive superbikes around today. They can typically reach speeds of up to 320km/h (200mph).

Superbike information is often top secret, so the statistics on these spreads are approximate.

999 R (Ducati, Italy, 2007)

- **Engine:** 999cc, inline 2 cylinder
- **Weight:** 181kg (399lbs)
- **Power:** 148bhp at 9,750rpm
- **Type:** racing superbike

Road superbikes rarely reach their highest speeds because those speeds are illegal on most public highways.

Hayabusa GSX1300R (Suzuki, Japan, 2010)

- **Engine:** 1,340cc, inline 4 cylinder
- **Weight:** 220kg (485lbs)
- **Power:** 172bhp at 9,500rpm
- **Type:** road superbike

1190 RC8 (KTM, Austria, 2010)

- **Engine:** 1,148cc, V2
- **Weight:** 184kg (406lbs)
- **Power:** 152bhp at 10,000rpm
- **Type:** racing superbike

This style of motorbike is raced at a Superbike World Championship event known as Superstock 1000.

CBR1000RR Fireblade (Honda, Japan, 2011)

- **Engine:** 999cc, inline 4 cylinder
- **Weight:** 199kg (439lbs)
- **Power:** 176bhp at 12,500rpm
- **Type:** road superbike

RSV4 (Aprilia, Italy, 2010)

- **Engine:** 1,000cc, V4
- **Weight:** 184kg (406lbs)
- **Power:** 241bhp at 12,500rpm
- **Type:** racing superbike

Italian racer Max Biaggi won the Superbike FIM World Championship in 2010, riding an Aprilia RSV4.

Organized racing involves different events for sport bikes and superbikes depending on their engine capacity. The championships involve many rounds of races at different racetracks around the world.

S 1000 RR (BMW, Germany, 2010)

- **Engine:** 999cc, inline 4 cylinder
- **Weight:** 183kg (403lbs)
- **Power:** 193bhp at 13,000rpm
- **Type:** racing superbike

To help make them extra light, some racing superbikes, such as this Moto Guzzi, don't have headlights or mirrors.

MGS-01 Corsa (Moto Guzzi, Italy, 2010)

- **Engine:** 1,225cc, V2
- **Weight:** 192kg (423lbs)
- **Power:** 128hp at 8,000rpm
- **Type:** racing superbike

YZR-M1 (Yamaha, Japan, 2010)

- **Engine:** 998cc, inline 4 cylinder
- **Weight:** 148kg (326lbs)
- **Power:** 200bhp at 12,500rpm
- **Type:** racing superbike

Spanish racer Jorge Lorenzo won the 2010 MotoGP World Championship riding a Yamaha YZR-M1.

Dirt bikes

Dirt bikes are rugged machines that are used in off-road races, Speedway, Motocross, and ice and endurance races.

Dirt bikers often stand up when riding.

Frames made of light metals, such as chromium or aluminium, keep the bikes fast.

RXV 4.5 (Aprilia, Italy, 2006)

- **Engine:** 449cc, V2
- **Weight:** 122kg (269lbs)
- **Power:** 60bhp at 13,000rpm

Small fuel tanks carry enough to race but not so much that the heavy fuel slows them down.

E2 250 EXC-F (KTM, Austria, 2010)

- **Engine:** 250cc, single cylinder
- **Weight:** 96kg (212lbs)
- **Power:** 38bhp at 13,500rpm

Knobbly tyres give grip over gravel, stones or mud.

Off-road races called trials, on muddy or rocky courses, test a biker's ability and a bike's performance.

This biker, Martin Barr, is taking part in an off-road trial as part of the 2009 European MX2 Motocross Championships.

Notice the goggles that protect the rider's eyes from the soil and dust. Find out more about Motocross on pages 48-49.

This Speedway event took place at the Millennium Stadium, Cardiff, in the UK, in 2003.

Speedway

Speedway is a fast and popular type of track racing, using modified dirt bikes. Two teams, with two riders each, race around the course four times. The riders earn points depending on their finishing place.

Speedway bikes run on a chemical called methanol, not petrol. Methanol lets them accelerate really quickly, but is more expensive than petrol.

When the race is over, the riders let go of the throttle and put their feet on the ground to stop.

Each team competes in 15 races at a day-long event. At the end, the team with the most points wins.

Start and finish line

The race is around an oval-shaped, dirt-surfaced track.

Padded crash barriers, called air fences, surround the track.

Audience seating

Motocross

Motocross is a popular type of off-course racing. It involves riding dirt bikes around courses with dirt, mud or grass surfaces. Along the route, there are hills to climb, ledges to jump from and obstacles to avoid.

Riders climb a steep hill while competing in a British Motocross Championship race in Wiltshire, in the UK, in 2010.

One type of Motocross event takes place at indoor stadiums and is called Supercross. 20 riders race for 20 laps around courses that include man-made ramps and jumps.

Motocross was originally called scrambling. Now a scramble usually means a race through a wooded area, slipping and sliding along muddy paths and around trees and hedges.

Ice racing

Ice racing is slippery and dangerous. Ice racing bikes are fitted with spiked tyres that dig into the surface for balance.

These riders are taking part in the Team Ice Racing World Championship final in the Netherlands.

Ice racing bikes use methanol as fuel.

The tyre spikes give the bikes more grip as they take corners. They might slip and slide, but they still keep going at average speeds of about 115km/h (70mph).

Most races are held on oval shaped tracks on the icy surfaces of frozen lakes or on winding, snow-covered roads. But some are held at indoor tracks.

The championships were first held in 1979. The 2010 winner was Russia. They won every year from 2003 to 2010.

The Dakar Rally

The ultimate off-road journey, that tests a rider's strength, skill and determination over a number of days, is known as an endurance race. The most famous one for motorbikes is the Dakar Rally.

Riders race across the Atacama Desert during the 2010 Dakar Rally in South America. The race also involves riding over steep mountains, along coastal roads and through water.

The Dakar is about 9,000km (5,600 miles) long. It starts in late December and lasts 16 days. Some days the bikers cover 800 - 1,000km (500 - 600 miles) over 12 hours of intense riding.

The Dakar Rally gets its name from the city of Dakar in Senegal where most of the rallies used to finish.

START
PARIS
France

Spain

Ferry from Spain to Morocco.

Morocco

Mauritania

Senegal
DAKAR
FINISH

But since 2009 the rally organizers have chosen routes through South America, instead – although the race is still called the Dakar Rally.

ARICA

Chile

Argentina
BUENOS AIRES

START and FINISH

Doing the Dakar

It takes months to prepare for the Dakar Rally. Riders go to the gym to exercise to get fit before race training.

Jacket with built-in water bottle and straw

Then they need to get 'bike fit' – able to ride all day long. Riders enter day long endurance tests to train, riding through mud, over sand and up mountains.

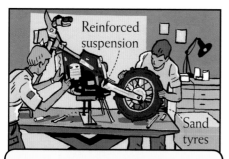

Reinforced suspension

Sand tyres

Dirt bikes are modified to cope with the race length and conditions.

BRRRMMM!   BRRRMMM!

The race begins early in the morning. When everyone turns on their engines at the start line, the noise is deafening.

Road book

Each day of the rally is broken into stages. The riders navigate the route by following directions from a road book.

Rally cars and huge trucks also enter the race. But, they cause huge dust clouds which reduce visibility.

Some riders have support teams of mechanics, who travel separately and repair the bikes each night. Other riders must fix their bikes themselves before they sleep.

The Dakar camp is known as a bivouac and it moves with the race. It's a small town of tents, medical staff, mechanics and organisers. Each day huge planes transport the bivouac to the next night's stop.

Some racers crash, become exhausted or get lost. Rescue helicopters can find them using positioning signals.

Only about a third of the riders make it to the end of the Dakar. They are all awarded medals for the acheivement.

How motorbikes began

Almost as soon as bicycles were first invented in the 19th century, engineers began thinking of how to adapt them into powered vehicles.

The larger front wheel was still powered by pedals.

A fire boiler turned water into steam to drive the back wheel.

No brakes

Michaux & Perraux (France, 1868)

A French bicycle company, Michaux and Perraux, designed a bicycle with a rear wheel that was powered by a steam engine.

Roper (USA, 1867)

An American designer, Sylvester Roper, also developed the idea of using a steam engine to power a bike.

Inside the saddle was a water tank. A lever was used to pump water to a boiler.

Brake lever

No pedals

The front wheel turned as the back wheel was powered by the engine.

Boiler

The first motorbike

In 1885, German inventors Gottlieb Daimler and Wilhelm Maybach created a bike powered by a new type of engine. Known as an internal combustion engine, it ran on petrol not steam. It's considered to be the first true motorbike.

Handlebars

Leather saddle

Wooden frame

Metal-rimmed wooden wheels

Footrest

Stabilizer wheel

Internal combustion engine

The story continues

After 1885, lots of engineers put forward their own ideas.
At first, many just added engines to their old bicycle designs.

Hildebrand & Wolfmüller
(Germany, 1894–1897)

Hildebrand & Wolfmüller
designed and produced
factory-built motorbikes to
sell to the public.

de Dion–Bouton (France, 1897)

A powered tricycle was designed
by the de Dion-Bouton company.
It was fast, but heavy and less
popular than lighter motorbikes.

Werner (France, 1897)

This bike, designed by the
Werner company, had the engine
positioned over the front wheel.
But this design made the bikes
unstable, so they tended to crash
and frequently caught fire, too.

Engine

Werner (France, 1900) — Engine

This Werner motorbike had its engine fitted to the frame between the wheels. It was a well balanced and very popular bike, but it had pedals in case the engine failed.

Early motorbike models were known by the company name and year. But, as more were designed, they were given their own names and codes.

Indian (USA, 1905)

This Indian was one of the first models where the rider started the engine by twisting the grips on the handlebars.

Triumph (UK, 1907)

This Triumph had a thicker metal frame and a bigger engine, but no pedals.

Harley-Davidson, Model 11J (USA, 1915)

This Harley-Davidson bike had heavy tyres and a V twin engine. The modern motorbike was beginning to develop.

Side-by-side

Motorbikes can be fitted with sidecars to carry
extra passengers. A sidecar is a specially designed
carriage with one wheel and no engine.

These riders are racing their bikes
and sidecars in an international
Motocross event in Germany.

This passenger is
hanging from the
sidecar to help keep
the bike balanced
during a turn.

Today, sidecars are mostly used by collectors and racers.
But they used to be quite common for everyday transport
in the days before many people owned cars.

Early sidecars

1915 Triumph Model H

Early sidecars were made of different materials, sold separately and attached to any bike.

Wicker sidecar

1954 Triumph T110 Swallow

Later sidecars were designed to match specific motorbikes and sold as a unit.

Bikes at war

During the First and Second World Wars, motorbikes were used as military vehicles. Unlike tanks and trucks, they could race over muddy battlefields and forests and scramble through war zones.

First World War 1914–1918

Douglas 2 (Douglas, UK, 1912–1922)

- **Engine:** 348cc, flat 2 cylinder
- **Top speed:** 64km/h (40mph)
- **Use:** Riders often carried battle updates, and orders, between soldiers and their generals.

Douglas produced around 70,000 military bikes during the First World War – more than any other manufacturer.

Two-tier side trolley to carry wounded soldiers

Indian Powerplus (Indian, USA, 1917)

- **Engine:** 984cc, V2
- **Top speed:** 100km/h (62mph)
- **Use:** Special ambulance side trolleys were used to carry wounded soldiers to medical tents.

Bikes in battle

Soldiers called despatch riders carried important paperwork and information from the front line.

Some sidecars carried homing pigeons. When the pigeons were released, they delivered messages to army headquarters.

Map of a typical First World War battlefield

Enemy front line trench

No man's land

Barbed wire

Support trench

Front line trench

Other sidecars carried mounted machine guns. The driver moved around, so that the gunman could aim at different enemy positions.

Ambulance bikes scrambled over battlefields. They were painted with a Red Cross sign so that the enemy knew they weren't a threat.

Royal Air Force (RAF) despatch riders leave an airfield in the UK to take part in an off-road training exercise, 1941.

Record breakers

The large, flat areas of the Bonneville Salt Flats, USA, are used by experts to ride specialized bikes. The ultra smooth surface helps them reach very high speeds of around 580km/h (360mph) in events known as land speed races.

This is the record breaking BUB Lucky 7 Streamliner bike.

The bike has a tube-shaped body instead of a simple metal frame.

The bike's two wheels are nearly 3m (10ft) apart.

The BUB Lucky 7 Streamliner set a new motorbike land speed record of 590km/h (367mph), in 2009 at Bonneville.

Dragsters

Dragsters are specially designed for use in drag races. A drag race involves two bikers racing along a straight course at speeds of up to 370km/h (230mph).

This dragster bike raced at the Thunderball Drag Race at the Santa Pod Raceway, UK, in 2009.

This dragster runs on nitromethane, an ultra-efficient, though sometimes dangerous, fuel. It's also fitted with a supercharger that sucks lots of air into the engine, making it extra powerful.

Second World War 1939–1945

Machine gun to be used by side-car passenger

KS750 (Zundapp, Germany, 1940–1948)

- **Engine:** 751cc, flat 2 cylinder
- **Top speed:** 96km/h (60mph)
- **Use:** In battle throughout Europe and in North Africa, on various different terrains.

2 man crew

Kettenrad (NSU & Stoewer, Germany, 1940–1948)

- **Engine:** 1,488 cc, inline 4 cylinder
- **Top speed:** 75km/h (46mph)
- **Use:** On snowy or sandy terrain to tow large guns and supplies.

3 man crew

Since the Second World War, small military trucks called jeeps have mostly replaced motorbikes in war.

Bike wheel

Tank tracks

Super stunts

Expert bikers perform amazing stunts, such as dramatic jumps, acrobatics and wheelies, in public displays.

The Royal Signals White Helmet Motorcycle Display Team started performing complicated motorbike acts in military shows in 1927.

This photograph, taken in 1991, shows members of the team performing a display for the public at the army base at Blandford Camp, Dorset, in the UK.

The rider lies down, rather than sitting on a saddle, following the streamlined shape of the bike. This isn't very comfortable, but the races are short.

This huge rear tyre is about four times wider than the front tyre. It helps the bike stay balanced at top speed.

Starting a drag race

A set of lights, called a Christmas Tree, flashes in sequence to count down to the start of a race.

1. As the bikes pull up to the start line, they break through an invisible detector beam. This triggers the lights.

2. The lights flash yellow, then amber, and finally the green lights signal the start.

The red bulbs only flash if there's a false start.

Detector beam

Some dragster bikes have rear wings to keep them travelling in a straight line.

This bike doesn't look anything like a usual motorbike. But it is defined as a bike in land speed record attempts because it has only two wheels.

Streamlined panelling

Cockpit

Rounded, aerodynamic nose

BUB
We make Pipes for Bikes!

Streamliner layout

The powerful V4, methanol-fuelled engine sits between the wheels in the middle of the bike's body.

The rider sits in the cockpit at the steering wheel.

6.4m (21ft)

Wall of Death

The Wall of Death is a famous stunt show. The audience stands at the top of a huge barrel-type stage.

Bikers ride at very high speeds around the bottom of the barrel. This creates a force that pushes them against the barrel wall, and lets them ride higher and higher without falling down.

The team is best-known for their balancing acts and fire jumps. They're consulted by film crews who are planning motorbike stunts for films, too.

This image was made using time-lapse photography. It combines shots of 17 different moments during a single jump.

Stunt story

Individual stunt riders often stage huge public events to show off their skills. They spend months rehearsing and assessing any dangers to try to make the stunt as safe as possible.

One of the most famous stunt riders was Evel Knievel (1938-2007). He broke 35 bones during his career, including his skull and lower back bone.

Stunt biker Travis Pastrana performed this complicated somersault routine at the 2004 X Games in Los Angeles, USA. The X Games is a series of international extreme sports competitions.

Classic bikes

Some bikers restore and ride stylish bikes from the 1930s, 1940s and 1950s, now known as classic bikes. They're often sleek and luxurious with strong, colourful designs and shiny engines.

Warrior (Indian, USA, 1949)

- **Engine:** 440cc, vertical twin
- **Weight:** 200kg (440lbs)
- **Power:** Unknown

Streamline KJ (Henderson, USA, 1930)

- **Engine:** 1,300cc, inline 4 cylinder
- **Weight:** 227kg (500lbs)
- **Power:** 40bhp at 4,000rpm

VLD (Harley-Davidson, USA, 1934)

- **Engine:** 1,200cc, V twin
- **Weight:** 185kg (408lbs)
- **Power:** 40bhp at 4,000rpm

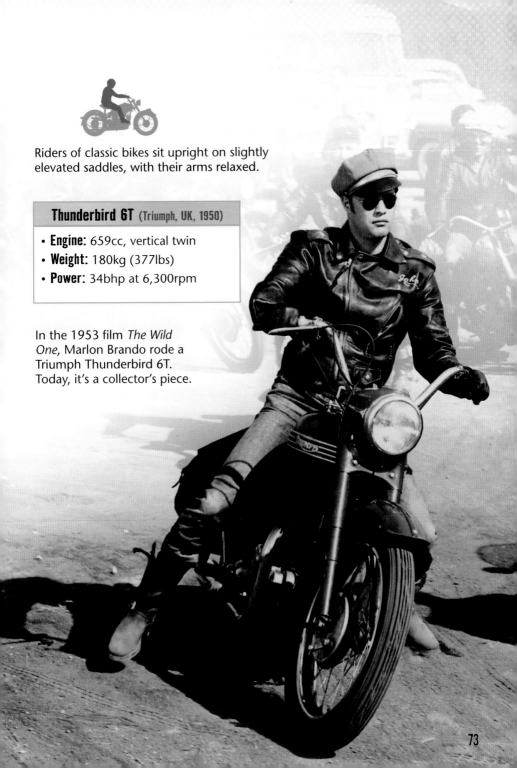

Riders of classic bikes sit upright on slightly elevated saddles, with their arms relaxed.

Thunderbird 6T (Triumph, UK, 1950)

- **Engine:** 659cc, vertical twin
- **Weight:** 180kg (377lbs)
- **Power:** 34bhp at 6,300rpm

In the 1953 film *The Wild One*, Marlon Brando rode a Triumph Thunderbird 6T. Today, it's a collector's piece.

Motorbikes on the internet

There are lots of exciting websites where you can find out more about motorbikes and see them in action. At the Usborne Quicklinks Website you'll find links to some great sites where you can:

- Explore a timeline of motorbikes.
- Watch video clips of the Dakar Rally.
- Learn more about how engines work.
- View clips of races and stunts.

For links to these sites and more, go to the Usborne Quicklinks Website at **www.usborne-quicklinks.com** and enter the keyword **motorbikes**.

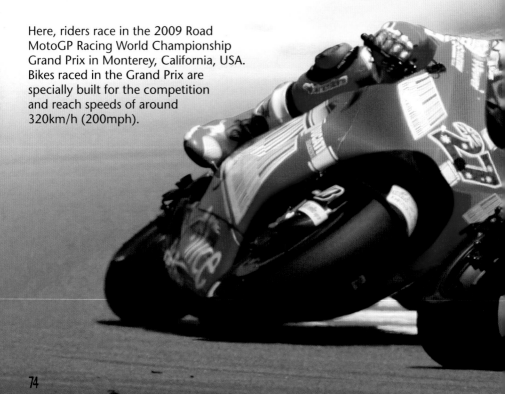

Here, riders race in the 2009 Road MotoGP Racing World Championship Grand Prix in Monterey, California, USA. Bikes raced in the Grand Prix are specially built for the competition and reach speeds of around 320km/h (200mph).

When using the internet please follow the internet safety guidelines displayed on the Usborne Quicklinks Website. The recommended websites in Usborne Quicklinks are regularly reviewed and updated, but Usborne Publishing Ltd. is not responsible for the content or availability of any website other than its own. We recommend that children are supervised while using the internet.

Glossary

The glossary explains some of the words used in this book.
Words in italics have their own entry.

acrobatic A type of *stunt* that involves the biker moving away from or around the bike in mid air before joining it again.

aerodynamic Designed with smooth sides to glide through air. Also known as *streamlined*.

bhp 'brake horse power', a unit to measure the power of an engine.

capacity The total amount of fuel and air drawn into the *cylinders* during one engine cycle, measured in cc or cubic centimetres.

carbon fibre A light, extremely strong material made out of incredibly thin fibres.

chassis The main body of a bike including the *frame*, wheels, *suspension* and brakes.

clutch The part that controls the connection between the engine and the *gearbox*.

counter steering Type of steering needed at high speeds. It involves turning the handlebars in the opposite direction to the turn.

crankshaft The part of an engine that turns the motion of the *pistons* into the rotation of the wheels.

cylinder The metal casing inside an engine that encloses a *piston*.

drag races Short races along straight courses ridden on bikes called dragsters.

drive system Part of the engine that uses power from the *gearbox* to turn the rear wheel.

endurance race A long race, that can last for days, that tests a rider's skill and determination.

exhaust Pipe that guides waste gases produced by the engine away from the motorbike.

fibreglass A strong, light material used for protective helmets.

fork Piece of metal that attaches the front wheel to the *frame*.

frame The skeleton of the bike – different sections of the frame are welded together to make it sturdy.

fuel injection system Part of a motorbike that mixes fuel with air, before they enter the engine

gearbox Part of the engine that controls the amount of power sent to the wheels from the engine.

internal combustion engine An engine that is powered by burning fuels such as petrol, diesel or methanol.

Kevlar Strong, tough man-made material resistant to scrapes and tears.

land speed record Races on specialized bikes to try to break the record for fastest land vehicle.

lap Once around a track or circuit.

mass-produced When a product is made in large numbers, in a factory.

methanol A liquid fuel that makes motorbikes go faster than petrol does.

off-road Riding or racing motorbikes on grass, mountains or mud.

panelling Plastic or metal trim that protects parts of machinery and can be decorative. Also known as fairing.

personaliszation Choosing a bike's design features to suit the rider's personal taste and style.

piston A solid piece of metal in an engine that moves up and down to power the bike.

positioning signals Computer and satellite system used to locate vehicles.

production line The sequence of assembly points in a factory where a motorbike is built.

rallying A competition in which bikers race from point to point and their times are recorded.

road race A motorbike race that takes place on public roads.

rpm 'revolutions per minute', a measure of how quickly the *crankshaft* spins and how powerful the engine is.

scooter A small, light and relatively inexpensive street motorbike.

sidecar A specially designed carriage that can be fixed to the side of a motorbike to carry passengers or luggage.

spokes Struts from the centre of a wheel to the rim.

steam engine An engine powered by the steam produced when water is boiled.

streamlined Designed with smooth sides to glide through air. Also known as *aerodynamic*.

stunt A trick, such as a jump, performed by a skilled motorbike rider.

suspension Part of a motorbike that deals with shocks and jolts to give a smooth ride.

track race A motorbike race that takes place on a purpose-built, enclosed course

tread pattern The pattern of grooves and marks in the tyre that aids grip.

visibility The ease with which a rider can see around him or her, which can be limited by bad weather, fog and sand storms.

wind tunnel A long room used for testing motorbikes. It has massive fans that simulate high-speed riding conditions.

Index

Page numbers marked with an 'a' are found underneath the flap on that page.

Acknowledgements

Every effort has been made to trace and acknowledge ownership of copyright. If any rights have been omitted, the publishers offer to rectify this in any future editions following notification. The publishers are grateful to the following individuals and organizations for their permission to reproduce material on the following pages: (b=bottom, r=right, l=left)

cover © actionplus sports images; **p1, p2-3, p45, p48-49** © Adam Duckworth; **p4 br** © Oleksiy Maysymenko/ Alamy; **p6** © JOHN G. MABANGLO/epa/Corbis; **p8-9** © Rick Friedman/Corbis; **p8a-9b** image supplied courtesy of Triumph Motorcycles Ltd.; **p10, p52-53** © JACKY NAEGELEN/Reuters/Corbis; **p13** image supplied courtesy of BMW Motorrad UK; **p18-19, p23** © Jacek Bilski/photolibrary.com; **p24** image supplied courtesy of Yamaha UK; **p26** image supplied courtesy of Kawasaki; **p28** © UK Emergency Vehicles, www.ukemergency.co.uk; **p30, p59 br** images supplied courtesy of Harley-Davidson Motorcycles; **p32-33** © Rick Chou/TRANSTOCK/ Transtock/Corbis; **p34-35** © A2 Wind Tunnel www.A2WT.com; **p36-37** © Getty Images; **p38-39** © Stringer/ Reuters/Corbis; **p41 br** © image supplied courtesy of Honda (UK) Motorcycles; **p46-47** © Jeff Morgan 08/Alamy; **p50-51** © actionplus sports images; **p57, p72** © Bettmann/CORBIS; **p60-61** © Guntmar Fritz/Corbis; **p64** © M. McNeill/Hulton Archive/Getty Images; **p66-67** © James Weishaar-D&W Images; **p66a-67a** © Leo Mason/Corbis; **p68-69** © Trinity Mirror/Mirrorpix/Alamy; **p70-71** © Bo Bridges/Corbis; **p74-75** © Konstandinos Goumenidis/Icon SMI/Corbis.

Motorbike illustrations p5 bl, p35 and p40-43 © Adrian Dean/F1ARTWORK

All other motorbike illustrations by John S Fox and www.avroart.com

Thanks for advice and additional research material to:
Tony Jakeman at BMW Motorrad UK, Carmela Piretti at Ducati, Mike Morgan at Harley-Davidson Motorcycles, Vivek Syal at Hero Honda, Honda (UK) Motorcycles, Marc Pomerantz at Indian Motorcycle Company, Khal Harris at Jardine International, Catherine Gonzalez at Kawasaki Motorcycles UK Ltd., Ross Walker at KTM UK, Kay Johnson at Norton Motorcycles Ltd., Daniela Riberti at Piaggio, Luke Plummer at Suzuki Motorcycles, Triumph Motorcycles Ltd. and Simon Belton at Yamaha UK. Special thanks also to Joshua Ansell.

Series editor: Jane Chisholm **Series designer:** Zoe Wray
Picture research: Ruth King **Digital design:** John Russell

First published in 2011 by Usborne Publishing Ltd., Usborne House, 83–85 Saffron Hill, London, EC1N 8RT, United Kingdom. www.usborne.com Copyright © 2012, 2011 Usborne Publishing Ltd. The name Usborne and the devices ♥ ⊕ are Trade Marks of Usborne Publishing Ltd. All rights reserved. No part of this publication may be reproduced, stored in any retrieval system, or transmitted in any form or by any means, electronic, mechanical, photocopying, recording or otherwise, without the prior permission of the publisher. UKE. Printed in Shenzhen, Guangdong, China.